CW00518391

BACON IN 3D

# BACON FACT

[
They say you can't buy
happiness, but you can buy
bacon. Which is pretty much
the same thing.
]

BACON IN 3D

# BACON
# WISDOM

[ It's a proven fact that all plans involving bacon have a 90% chance of working out. ]

# BACON QUOTE

> 66 You may have thought you heard me say I wanted a lot of bacon and eggs, but what I said was: Give me all the bacon and eggs you have. 99

– Ron Swanson

BACON IN 3D

# BACON CONFESSION

[
The only way I could love you
more is if you were wrapped
in bacon.
]

# BACON
# FACT

[ Bacon is the answer. I don't
remember the question. ]

BACON IN 3D

# BACON LYRICS

66 I like pig
butts and
I cannot
lie. 99

# BACON CONFESSION

[ I just want someone to look at
me the way I look at bacon. ]

# BACON
# POEM

[ Roses are red. Bacon is red.
Poems are hard. Bacon. ]

BACON IN 3D

# BACON QUOTE

66 I love the sound of rain pattering outside my window as I sleep. It sounds like bacon frying. 99

*– Unknown*

BACON IN 3D

# BACON TRUTH

[ Look, I can't make everyone
happy. I'm not bacon. ]

BACON IN 3D

# BACON WISDOM

[ Anything can be wrapped in bacon. ]

BACON IN 3D

# BACON QUOTE

**❝** Do you want
my leftover
bacon? **❞**

*– Said no one ever*

BACON IN 3D

# BACON TRUTH

[ Either you like bacon or
you're wrong. ]

BACON IN 3D

# BACON
# THREAT

[ If you try to pass off
turkey bacon as real bacon
one more time, I will find you
and I will kill you. ]

BACON IN 3D

# BACON LIFE

> 66 I'm so full.
> I couldn't eat
> another bite.
> Oh there's still
> bacon left?
> Ok... 99

# BACON WORKOUT

[ Yeah I lift....slices of bacon
into my mouth. ]

# BACON LOVE

[ Bacon is better than that chick
who said she would die for you.
Bacon actually died for you.
Bacon's love is real. ]

# BACON QUOTE

66 Mmmm ...
bacon 99

– *Homer Simpson*

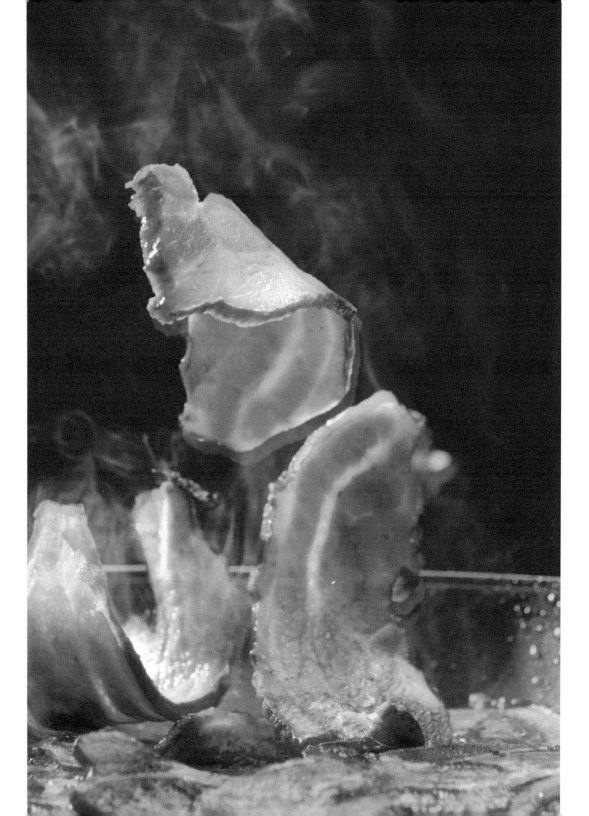

# BACON
# PICK-UP LINE

[
You can call me bacon
because your body makes me
*SIZZLE*
]

# BACON
# WISDOM

[
Bacon.
It's gonna save the world
someday. I don't know how...
but it will!
]

BACON IN 3D

# BACON QUOTE

66 I enjoy having breakfast in bed.
I like waking up to the smell of bacon,
sue me. And since I don't have a butler,
I have to do it myself. So, most nights
before I go to bed, I will lay six strips of
bacon out on my George Foreman grill.
Then I go to sleep. When I wake up, I plug
in the grill. I go back to sleep again. Then
I wake up to the smell of crackling bacon.
It is delicious, it's good for me, it's the
perfect way to start the day. 99

*– Michael Scott*

BACON IN 3D

# BACON CONFESSION

[ I once cried when I dropped bacon on the floor. No joke. ]

# BACON QUOTE

66 Bacon's the best.
Even the frying of
bacon sounds like
applause. 99

– Jim Gaffigan

BACON IN 3D

# BACON QUOTE

**66** Do you want to know how good bacon is? To improve other food, they wrap it in bacon! **99**

– Jim Gaffigan

BACON IN 3D

© 2017 SAM HOKE
All Rights Reserved

 @foodandpaws

Printed in Great Britain
by Amazon

43482255R00030